Cover Photo: Clear Yellow Border Canary.
Endpapers: Group of New Colored Canaries.

HOWELL

Beginner's guide to

Canaries

**Brian Robinson &
Scott Adams**

**Editor
Leonie Rudduck**

HOWELL BOOK HOUSE Inc.
230 Park Avenue
New York, N.Y. 10169

Library of Congress Cataloging-in-Publication Data

Robinson, Brian.
  Howell beginner's guide to canaries.

  Summary: A guide to caring for canaries as pets in the home.
  1. Canaries–Juvenile literature. [1. Canaries]
I. Adams, Scott. II. Title. III. Title: Beginner's guide to canaries.
SF463.R62 1985   636.6'862   85-21890
ISBN 0-87605-906-X

Photographs and illustrations © Paradise Press 1985
Paintings on PP. 18 & 19 by Peter Daley

Printed in Hong Kong through Bookbuilders Ltd

Contents

Introduction

In comparison with most other domesticated animal species the development of the canary has been achieved in a relatively short period of time - in fact, within the last 150 or so years. During that time most of the varieties and colors seen today have been produced by selective breeding - though the canary as a singing bird first became popular during the Middle Ages.

Origin

Following the Spanish conquest of the Canary Islands in the 15th century, many of the local races of singing finches were exported to Spain where they proved fashionable for ladies to own as pets. They were found to be lively and hardy cage birds that bred quite freely in captivity and soon established themselves as a profitable export market for the Spaniards, to other European countries as well as the West Indies. By selling only the cock birds, the Spanish held a monopoly on the trade for nearly a hundred years until a consignment destined for Italy escaped, or were freed, following a shipwreck. The birds were able to reach the Isle of Elba where they were captured by Italians who then bred and exported them. However, both sexes were sold and as a result, breeding populations were established all over Europe from whence present day varieties were to be developed.

Green Singing
Finches

The Wild Canary

The Serin Finch *(Serinus serinus)* is believed to be the species originally exported by the Spanish, which was to give rise to the canary *(Serinus canaria)*, and is indigenous to the Azores and Madeira as well as to the Canary Islands. The color of this bird is a dappled olive-green on its upper parts with a yellow-green below. Females are a duller, more brown, version of the males.

There are numerous species of serin finches including the Yellow-fronted Canary *(Serinus mozambicus)*, which is probably Africa's most popular cage-bird, and is well known in aviculture as the Green Singing Finch. The genus is one of many that comprise the finch family Fringillidae, which also includes the genus *Carduelis*. This is of particular interest to canary breeders as it contains the various siskin species one of which - the Black-hooded Red Siskin *(Carduelis or Spinis cucullatus)* - was used to hybridize with canaries and resulted in the Red Factor Canary.

The Pet Canary

Although originally kept for its song, selective breeding has resulted in many varieties over the years and, as a result, the canary became popular with people in all walks of life. By the turn of the 19th century they were the world's most numerous pet bird and it was not until the phenomenal growth in budgerigar breeding that they were finally toppled from their number one spot. Whilst the budgerigar still reigns in the popularity stakes the canary, none-the-less, is still bred in vast numbers - and there is every indication that the numbers are in fact increasing as more and more people come to know and enjoy the many attributes of these beautiful and sweet singing birds.

Canaries and Mines

It is doubtful if any other cage bird has ever been given such a life-saving role as was the first canary to enter a mine. Since that first bird, many millions have travelled deep into the earth as living detectors of poisonous gases. The birds reacted to such lethal gas long before the miners became aware of its presence, thus giving the men the chance to surface pending the clearance of the gas. Once the canaries stopped singing miners knew things were amiss: It is only in very recent years that these birds have been replaced with detecting equipment.

Societies

Any person about to acquire their first canary is well advised to join one of the many general or specialist societies that can be found throughout the country. Such clubs are promoted in the magazines such as *Cage and Aviary Birds* in the UK, or *Birdworld Magazine* in the USA. Alternatively, your local pet store or most breeders, will be able to supply addresses. The clubs can advise you on the finer points, help out on problems and direct you to other owners in your area who share your interest in these birds.

1. Varieties of Canaries

Looking around a canary show one could be excused for not believing the many varieties available were all bred from the one species of wild bird. With the exception of the New Colored Canaries, and certain infertile hybrids, it is none-the-less a fact. By selective breeding, and retention of mutations as they appeared, the canary fancy has developed birds ranging from the small Glosters to the tall Yorkshires.

To the average person, a canary is a yellow bird that sings well and it is only when they enquire further that they begin to appreciate the considerable diversity of type, color and markings that may be purchased. If your need is purely for a pretty song bird then the Border Canary is likely to measure up to your concept of what a pet should be. However, if you wish to keep a number of canaries, or plan to breed and exhibit, then more detailed information will be needed on the various varieties and the degree of difficulty in keeping them.

Types of Canaries

Most canary breeders will have a special interest in one of three differing types of canary, these being: those bred for their shape, referred to as 'type' birds; those kept for their song; those bred for their color. Whilst a fancier may keep more than one of these loose groupings, he will invariably develop a bias to specialization. Many breeders devote their entire interest to one specific variety, which they support with tremendous devotion. It can be seen that the beginner, regardless of their preference, will find many people within the fancy that have much the same levels of interest as they do. The above said, the newcomer should not think that because one likes 'type' birds that song or color will be sacrificed. All canary varieties are excellent singers but a Roller is outstanding; all canaries are colorful but the New Color Canaries are especially so, and all canaries are well shaped but many are quite unmistakable.

Terminology

Unless you require any other than a pet bird, the chances are that you will need to contact a breeder. If the variety you are interested in is not available locally, you will be purchasing through mail advertisements. This so, a need to understand such terms as 'unflighted', 'buff', 'variegated' or 'corona' will be essential if you are to build up a mental picture of what is on offer.

Border Canary -
the most popular
variety

Color

Canaries are basically yellow birds on which black and brown pigment is superimposed, which results in a whole range of shades depending on the degree of the color combinations. The yellow can range from very pale to a deep dark shade, and if no black or brown is present such birds are described as *clear*. The depth of the color can be changed by color feeding during the molt. At the opposite end of the color range to the *clear* is the *self*, which is a bird with no light feathering showing through. The visual effect of this is green. Where brown is imposed on the yellow the result is a cinnamon color which appeared as a mutation. White also appeared as a mutation and the effect of black and brown on it is to produce a slate-blue color whilst brown on white produces fawn. White canaries can be found in most varieties. Red Factor and New Color canaries are discussed under their relative headings.

Variegation

The way in which black and brown is superimposed on a bird is known as variegation. It is used to describe all birds between the clear yellow (or white) and the green (or blue). Where a bird has irregular patches of dark and light feathers all over its body it is said to be *variegated*. If the bird has only one small patch of dark feathers on an otherwise clear body it is described as *ticked*. Conversely, if there are a few light feathers on a dark bird it is said to be *fouled*.

10

The Gloster Fancy Canary. This is an example of the corona type.

Whilst most canary feathers are uniformly yellow, they can sometimes be tipped with white - where the pigment has not extended to the full length of the shaft. Such feathers present a softer, almost frosted, appearance and are termed *buff*. These feathers are also somewhat larger and wider, thus giving the bird a more bulky appearance. Where birds are described as *crested* this means they sport a round rosette of feathers on their heads - it should, ideally, radiate from a central spot and be even all round. In the case of the Gloster canary the crest is called a *corona*. Whilst the normal canary head is termed a *plain-head*, in the Gloster it is called a *consort*. Lizard canary heads are referred to as *caps*. Birds are referred to as 'unflighted' when they are under one year old. During their first molt a bird will shed only its body feathers and not until its second molt are the wing and tail feathers shed and replaced with new ones - at which point the bird is described as 'flighted'.

'Type' Canaries

The Gloster Fancy

This variety was first seen in London in 1925 and is named in honor of Mrs. Rogerson of Cheltenham, Gloucestershire, England, who was its creator. It was developed by crossing crested Roller Canaries with small Borders. Infusions of Crested Canary genes were also introduced in order to create

11

what is now the smallest, and probably the second most popular, canary. It should be no more than 11.5cm (4½in.) in length, neat and 'cobby' in stature and its crest should not extend over its eyes. When being bred, corona should be paired with consort to retain quality of the crest because corona to corona will yield a percentage of dead in the shell chicks. Although yellow x buff is the ideal mating this may present problems as, through bad breeding years ago, the availability of yellows is somewhat restricted. It is a delightful canary that is an easy breeder, reasonably priced, ideal for beginners and does not require color feeding.

The Border Canary

Originally known as the Cumberland, the Border Canary officially came into being in 1890, and was developed from local varieties in Northern England and the Scottish border counties. It is a small bird with a maximum length of 14cm (5½in.) and should appear rounded from any position. Feathering is a most important aspect, and these should be fine and smooth, with no tendency to coarseness. The bird should be very lively at all times and, because of this, potential show birds must be trained from a very early age. The Border is probably the most popular of all canaries and certainly the most exhibited bird. The variety is not color fed but attention to diet during molting is essential in all non color fed birds in order to bring out the very best natural color. Always breed yellow to buff. Highly recommended for beginners, the Border is seen in all the accepted colors.

The Norwich Canary is gaining new devotees all the time.

The modern Yorkshire Canary is of mixed heritage and is far more stocky than the slim birds seen decades ago.

The Norwich Canary

Formerly the most popular variety, the Norwich lost many supporters following the introduction of larger varieties to increase its size in the 1920's. This resulted in what are known as feather 'lumps' which are cysts at the feather base. Though the cysts are now largely a thing of the past, the variety has never regained its former position and probably ranks third. They were the first canaries to be color fed and can be many shades ranging from yellow through to deep orange. A cinnamon variety has been known for many years and may well have been the first canary mutation. They are judged for their color, which receives considerably more points than in the normal Norwich. The variety should not exceed 16cm (6¼in.) and is a broad, thick set bird. It is not lively, like the Border, nor elegant in movement as is the Yorkshire, but that is not to suggest it should ever be slow or sluggish. They are not the easiest birds to breed from a beginner's standpoint, and the range of colors will be found more restrictive. Prices will be quite expensive for good birds.

The Yorkshire Canary

This variety of canary is of a very mixed heritage and is not really recommended for the beginner. It is regarded as being the 'gentleman or soldier' of the fancy due to its elegant erect stance. Originally a very slim bird, it is now more stocky and somewhat 'carrot-shaped'. In length it is 17cm (6¾in.) making it one of the largest varieties. It is color fed and seen in most

An outstanding example of a Cinnamon Buff cock Border Fancy Canary.

available shades. It is essential that it has long legs and that its back to tail line be as straight as possible - wings should not over-lap (known as scissoring) but lay flat. Yorkshires are very expensive birds and show training will be very time consuming. Very much a connoisseur's choice.

The Lizard Canary

This is the oldest known variety of canary and, as it is judged entirely on its feather pattern, it is arguably not a 'type' canary. This pattern is a series of black spots, which extend down the back and sides to the tail root, and are termed 'spangles' - they are the most important feature of the bird. Length is about 12cm (4¾in.) and in shape they resemble a Border canary. It may be noticed that they are the only 'type' variety not named after a locality, which is because this is not known, being lost in antiquity. The variety is found in just two colors, these being Gold (yellow in other varieties) and Silver (buff in other varieties). The cap is a feature of the breed and it may be clear or 'broken'. There are many other terms unique to the variety which the novice will need to learn. They can be recommended to beginners because they are good breeders and there is considerable scope for exhibition success - they will appeal to those who want a real challenge.

Other 'Type' Canaries

The five varieties so far discussed are likely to be those from which most beginners will select their first birds. There are, however, numerous other 'type' birds which may be available - depending on locality. In the UK the *Fife Fancy* was developed in Scotland in the 1950's and is well supported there. It

A superb study of an evenly marked
White Yorkshire Canary

is a miniature Border canary not exceeding 11.5cm (4½in.). In total contrast, the *Lancashire Coppy* was one of the largest ever canaries at around 19cm (7½in.). It became extinct during the Second World War but is being 're-created' as the genes are still available in the many varieties in which the original Lancashires were progenitors.

There are numerous canaries known as 'Frills', which are characterized by feathers which curl in various directions. Examples of frilled canaries are the *Dutch*, which was the original, the *Parisian*, the *Padovan*, the *Milan* and the *Gibber Italicus*. These canaries, often regarded as oddities, are not generally popular other than in Continental Europe. One canary that has had considerable influence in the formation of numerous other breeds is the *Belgian Fancy* canary. In its normal stance it appears slightly humpbacked, but in a show stance it is quite unmistakeable with its head pointing down to the cage bottom and neck fully extended. It is one of the very oldest varieties and was used in creating Lancashires, Yorkshires, Frills, and the *Scotch Fancy*. The latter is a very similar bird and is enjoying somewhat of a resurgence in the UK at this time. The *Columbus Fancy* is one of the very few home-bred American canaries and is seen as both crest and plain head. A number of British breeds went into its development and as a result 'type' can be difficult to maintain. It is about 14.6cm (5¾in.) in length, cobby in body and the crest, if appropriate, is its most important feature.

Singing Canaries

The Roller Canary
It is to fanciers in the Hartz mountains of Germany that the Roller's origins can be traced. The birds were, and still are, bred exclusively for their singing ability. The size, shape or color of a Roller canary is of no importance whatsoever and, as a result, most look like the original wild birds, being generally selfs with occasional variegated specimens being seen.

The song of the Roller is quite different from that of any other variety, it being a continuous delivery of notes that are more melodious and flowing. Rollers are judged on the way they perform song passages, called 'tours'; a good bird will put a number of these together in such a way that it progresses from one to the other in smooth transition, varying in volume, and rising or falling in note to form a complete musical composition. A really good song bird is the result of many years of line and strain breeding as well as of careful attention to training.

It is not possible to buy a Roller from the local pet shop (other than a breeder reject) simply because they must be kept away from all other bird sounds. Their song is developed, from a young age, by mimicry of an adult bird referred to as a 'teacher'. Such birds are placed with a number of youngsters in a birdroom and by careful selection of those that attain the desired standard of 'rolls' and 'tours' so the song is passed from generation to generation. Any that fail to produce the right notes, though excellent birds by any other standard of singing, are not retained by good Rollermen. It is possible to use tape-recordings of winning Roller's repertoires in place of 'teachers' but, unless the quality of the tape - and of the output equipment - is excellent, then there is always the risk of 'students' picking up undesired sounds.

Roller contests cannot be held in conjunction with normal 'type' bird shows so you will need to visit a specialist Roller meeting to see and hear stock. This is clearly essential as it is the only way one can hope to appreciate the quality of song needed. You will also need to know what constitutes the sounds of the thirteen tours that make up the British Standard. In the USA and Canada, an alternative system, known as the One Hundred Point Standard, may be used for judging, and each show will announce which standard is to be used.

The American Singer Canary
This songster was developed to meet the needs of Americans who wanted both a 'type' bird, that would have good appeal to pet-lovers, yet would have a better than average singing ability. The ideal, laid down by the standard, should be a bird that is 69% Roller and 31% Border Fancy. It should be no more than 14.6cm (5¾in.) in length and deliver its song whilst perched (whereas a Roller will sing whilst moving). The Singer is not as popular as the Roller but the ranks of its followers grows each year. They are judged against their own National Standard.

Breeding Song Canaries
Whether you have Rollers or the American Singer it is only the cocks that sing but the hens are of equal importance in passing on the ability. By keeping careful records of the best songsters, breeders are able to trace which hens are clearly producing top quality cocks. If you are at all interested in particular colors in canaries you will find that the 'singing varieties' are not for you because, sooner or later, you will have to compromise and, especially in Rollers, that is a totally unacceptable word; for Rollermen, it is song or nothing! You should purchase either variety from a reputable source — buy the best you can afford — for it is only in this way that you can start from a foundation of known quality songsters.

New Colored Canaries

Within the last fifty-five years the canary fancy has witnessed its biggest phenomenon - the development of the new colored canaries. Strictly speaking, this 'variety', or group, is not really one of true canaries because they are the result of crossings with another species thus they are, more correctly, fertile hybrids. However, as they freely interbreed with all canary varieties they have become an integral party of the hobby. For years, breeders had desired to introduce other colors into the canary and Dr. Hans Duncker, a German geneticist, published a thesis in 1929 in which he felt a red canary was possible by crossings with the Hooded Siskin *(Carduelis or Spinus cucullatus)* of Venezuela. He was right - well almost.

The red of the siskin was thought to be a single gene but it proved otherwise,

Clear
Yellow
Norwich

Scots
Fancy

Canary Varieties

Broken-cap
Lizard

Dutch
Frill

Clear-cap
Lizard

Light Siskin
x Canary

Canary Hybrids

Canary
x Bullfinch

Greenfinch
x Canary

and was the result of multi-gene action. When, eventually, fertile hybrids were well established and crossed back to canary hens, an orange-red was produced. This was because both red *and* yellow were passed from siskins to the yellow canaries. None-the-less, the breakthrough had been achieved and Red Factor canaries had arrived. Since those days a true red is still sought but breeders, by careful selection, have come a long way towards that goal. In recent years new mutations have appeared and have resulted in over fifty colors being recognised from gray to copper and from rose to bronze. The birds are color-fed during and after their molt and whilst this is standard procedure a number of eminent judges, such as George Lynch, feel this defeats the object of color breeding on the very sound principle that true 'natural' colored birds are often beaten in competition by birds whose color is more artificial than real. Color is the sole criteria within this group though, with so many shades now firmly established, type is becoming more sought after. Beginners are recommended to visit canary shows in order to see the available range and to discuss breeding with fanciers in this area of the hobby as it is quite complex. The birds themselves are good breeders and feathering is both of the normal and frosted varieties. It is quite possible to introduce any of the new colors into the standard 'type' varieties but is seldom done as ardent breeders are, quite naturally, cautious at introducing genes that could adversely effect 'type'. The Red Factor and New Colored Canary devotees are, in Continental Europe, found in greater numbers than all other varieties put together, whilst in both the UK and USA their numbers are substantial.

Mules

The term mule is generally applied to any offspring resulting from the mating of a canary with any other species. Such offspring have always proven, with one exception, to be infertile. We have seen how this type of experimental breeding resulted in the new colored canaries but it is practised as a hobby in itself and, especially in the UK, has a great number of followers. There are classes at exhibitions for such birds. The availability of stock can be more expensive than with canaries simply because the birds are 'one offs' and because, in most countries, it is illegal to own indigenous species unless they are closed rung. This clearly limits breeding stock.

Among the more popular crossings are with Goldfinch, the Linnet, the Greenfinch, the Siskin, the Redpoll and the Twite. The first two named produce beautiful singing birds - the rules for teaching the song are the same as for Rollers. Generally, Norwich (or Norwich bred) hens are mated to the other species, and yellow feathered birds will tend to produce more attractive offspring than buff feathered. However, in the breeding of mule and hybrid birds there are no rules. Most mules prove to be hardier pets than canaries, are longer lived and, if properly 'taught', will have better singing ability - which they will sustain for longer periods and even during their molts is not unheard of.

The great appeal of this aspect of canary keeping lies in the unexpected - one never quite knows what will turn up if the mating is successful, and the challenge of making a 'first' known pairing is very real. On the negative side, the number of failures will be high. Certainly would-be beginners should approach this area of the hobby with great caution, and should visit shows and discuss problems with experienced fanciers before embarking into it.

Recommendations

It is a fact of life that all beginners will be advised to buy this or that variety because it is an easy breeder. They will likewise be warned from starting with a given breed because of its problems - this book is no different on these accounts, but the novice should be aware of numerous reasons *why* people give recommendations - which are not always because of difficulty in actually keeping or breeding a specific variety. Often, on analysis, recommendations prove to be totally incorrect, because much depends on the reasons for which you wanted the birds in the first place. As an example, many people 'warn-off' beginners from Lizard canaries on the grounds that the spangling effect is difficult to get right - which is true. However, if a novice were to start breeding and exhibiting Lizards his chances of show success would be greater than if he started in the most popular breed - Borders. The latter fancy has considerable numbers in it who have devoted years to perfecting their stock, so competition will be really fierce. Breeding an outstanding Border is no easier than producing a top Lizard — the number of 'failed' Border breeders is proof of this! The limited 'gene pool' in Lizards means that novices have almost as good a chance of coming up with a good bird as a seasoned campaigner. Sure, the spangling is a challenge — but do not think the stance of a Yorkshire or the crest of a Norwich will prove to be a pushover.

You are more likely to be recommended to popular breeds because there are more people keeping them - each wanting to sell you stock. They will often decry less popular birds, though never having owned them themselves. On more valid grounds, recommendation may be based on price or availability. The fancier in Brisbane or South Dakota may not be able to obtain a Fife Fancy nor the Londoner an American Singer. Books will tend to recommend those varieties that are easily located and reasonable in price. The Novice should always try to speak with people *in* the variety that appeals and then balance this with all other considerations before making a final choice - if there just is no one in your area with your choice maybe you should become the first!

2. Housing

The obvious decision to be made before buying a canary is how the bird will be housed - and this will depend, in part, on whether you just want a pet bird or intend to breed canaries. For pet canaries a standard commercial bird cage will be ideal - and the larger the cage the better, as adequate exercise is most important. Canary fanciers have a wider choice of cage than do keepers of budgerigars or other parrots, because with canaries there is no risk of the bird eating its way out of wooden or plastic cages. Although the many attractive and ornate wooden or bamboo cages will adequately accommodate canaries, they are often far more difficult to keep clean than all-metal or plastic cages, - apart from invariably being very small.

Possibly the most suitable bird cage - but one which is not as aesthetically attractive as many commercially available cages - can be made quite simply using a wooden box and fitting a metal cage front, available at pet and hardware stores, plus a metal floor tray. This type of cage offers a number of advantages, additional to the cost-saving, over cages which have open bars all around. Chills, through drafts, are less likely and timid birds are given a sense of security by being able to back off into a solid corner. A disadvantage is the greater difficulty in thorough cleansing, and the ability of mites to hide in corners and cracks. If this type of cage - or any wooden cage - is chosen, extra care must be taken with cleaning programs.

Perches, Feeding Pets and Bathing

Perches should be placed at varying heights and distances so the bird exercises its wings as it flits around the cage and ideally they should be of several thicknesses so the bird's feet are exercised as it grasps the perches - which should be oval, rather than round, in shape. Unlike budgerigars, canaries are rarely interested in plastic cage toys. A swing, though, will usually prove attractive to a canary. The bird may also use a plastic ladder. Take care not to clutter the cage to such an extent that the bird has little room to move.

The cage should be fitted with food and water dishes, and these should be located in such a way as to prevent them being fouled by the bird's droppings, as will surely happen if the dishes are placed beneath a perch. Plastic hoppers, which usually feature a clear glass tube emptying into a flat tray, are ideal for both food and water. They can be placed near a perch without the danger of fouling. The clear plastic tubes enable you to check at a glance that the bird has a plentiful supply of seed or water, and many styles are designed so the tray pushes through the cage wire while the hopper tube remains clipped to the outside of the cage, allowing simple removal, cleaning and refilling.

Canaries love to bathe, particularly in warm weather, so you should make provision for this. A number of commercial bird baths are available - even battery-operated bird showers which pump water from a small reservoir when the bird activates a switch by standing on the shower perch. A simpler bird bath can be a shallow dish partly filled with water and placed on the cage floor. Bird baths which clip onto the outside of the cage door are preferable because they stop the cage from becoming too wet through the bird splashing as it bathes.

Hygiene

The cage you choose should be fitted with a removable metal floor tray. This will make cage cleaning simpler. A sand or shellgrit covered floor sheet - often sold in pet shops as "health sheets" - should be placed on the tray. The sheet's rough surface will help to keep the bird's feet free of fouling by droppings and during cleaning the sheet can be simply removed and replaced. Similar grit covered brown paper is available for use as perch covers, and this also serves the dual purpose of making cleaning easier and keeping the bird's feet healthier. Clean white paper can also be used to cover cage floors, but newspaper is not suitable as the ink tends to make the bird's feathers dirty.

Plastic cage surrounds can be bought to stop feathers, seed husks or droppings escaping from the cage and making a mess beneath it. A cage cover,

One of the many New Color Canaries, this Bronze male clearly shows his Siskin heritage

to place over the cage at night, can either be bought ready-made or fashioned from a piece of cloth. Cage covers are necessary if the bird is expected to sleep in a room where lights are turned on after dark, or if car headlights or street lights are apt to shine through windows and disturb, or perhaps frighten, the bird.

Before being used, the cage should be thoroughly scrubbed with a good detergent and disinfectant. This is equally important whether the cage is brand new or if it has had a previous owner. A new cage must be scrubbed to remove any dangerous chemicals left during the manufacturing process, while a used cage - particularly one where the fate of the previous occupant is unknown - must be thoroughly cleansed to ensure no diseases or parasites are present to endanger the new bird's health. During the cleaning the cage should be checked to ensure there are no loose or sharp pieces which could injure the bird and no paint flakes which could poison it.

Cage Location

Siting of a cage is most important for the happiness and health of the bird it contains. The room should be light and airy - but the cage's location must be free of drafts or extremes of heat and cold. The bird must be safe in its cage, out of danger from cats and away from the reach of children who could overturn the cage and let the bird escape. Windows often allow frosts and chills to strike through them, while the glass can also magnify heat, so the cage must not be constantly positioned too close to these. Extreme heat can cause a canary to go into a form of molt which will stop it singing and could eventually kill it - yet canaries like some sunlight and thrive in temperatures of between 60 and 70 degrees Fahrenheit (between 16 and 21 degrees Celsius).

As canaries are very sensitive to noxious vapors the cage must be sited in an area where they are in no danger from escaping gas from cooking appliances or heaters. Care must also be taken not to allow too much tobacco smoke near the bird, and gasoline fumes, exhaust gases and fresh paint fumes must be avoided at all cost. A location free from artificial light after sundown is ideal, as then the bird's sleep will not be disturbed. A shelf against a wall, or a hook on a wall, is a good cage location as the wall offers the bird some protection, but a well-sited stand and cage is suitable, provided it is steady and well located.

Aviaries and Breeding Cages

Canaries are ideal as aviary subjects, provided the aviary is well constructed, well located and safe. If other birds are kept with the canaries these must be of compatible type so no conflict arises. A suitable aviary is one which offers protection from the weather, plenty of flying space and freedom from vermin. Shrubs and bushes can add to the appearance of an aviary as well as offer the birds shelter and natural surroundings. Unlike parrots, the canaries will do little damage to either plants or fittings.

Provided they are kept in a sufficiently large area canaries are easy to breed in cages. The minimum breeding area would be about 60cm long, 30cm wide and 45cm high (24in x 12in x 18in). The breeding cage should be placed in a well-sheltered place, away from any likely disturbances and should also contain nests and nesting materials.

Many breeders use double wooden cages, fitted with a slide-in partition board to separate the two halves of the cage when necessary. Such breeding cages can be bought in many pet shops or made from boxes and wire cage fronts. Serious canary fanciers, who breed large numbers of birds either for showing or sale, generally have bird rooms - with ample natural light and air filled with breeding cages and open flight cages for young birds and 'resting' breeding stock. Although large numbers of birds can be bred in aviaries, this 'colony' breeding method does not allow the breeder anywhere near the same control as does a cage breeding situation.

Because show birds must have perfect plumage, it is best if they do not need to be handled when entering the show cage, so as soon as they feel confident in the new cage they are taught to enter it when directed, using a piece of thin wood or a training stick to guide them initially. Next, the show cage is taken away from the bird's holding cage while the bird being trained is inside. Gentle handling, and a reassuring voice, quickly calms any immediate fright the bird has and it soon learns there is nothing to fear in the show cage.

The most time consuming part of the training comes next, as the young bird learns to pose in the correct stance for its variety. This is done by attracting the bird's attention then encouraging it to hold the position for as long as possible. Serious exhibitors next accustom their birds to artificial lighting, unusual noises, and strange movements so they will remain in position while being judged. The efforts these people put into training their birds is often rewarded when prizes are announced at a show.

Pet Canaries

There are no set guidelines for training a pet canary - it is too much a matter of personal choice and depends largely on the time and effort the owner is prepared to expend. The first step, though, is to tame the bird so it looks on its owner as a friend, and this is a fairly simple process, just a matter of patiently and gently winning the bird's confidence. Like most birds, canaries have an instinctive fear of sudden movements, particularly movements above their heads. To overcome this you should ensure all actions you take near your bird are slow and deliberate. Your bird will soon learn that you mean it no harm and as it becomes increasingly relaxed with you your movements can become more natural. In a short time the bird will accept any normal behaviour you display - although sudden loud noises or unusual activity may set it fluttering.

Canaries can be permitted to fly freely about a room once they are tamed and care is taken to ensure all windows, doors, vents and chimneys are closed to

The extinct Lancashire Coppy Canary is now being revived by carefull selective breeding

prevent escape. Heaters, stoves and fans must also be switched off and potential dangers such as dogs and cats should not be present. To avoid distressing the bird by having to capture it to return it to its cage, it is wise to teach it to perch on your hand before releasing it. Start this lesson by removing all perches from the cage, then slowly place your finger inside and coax the bird to perch on it. This often takes some time, but if you keep your finger as low as possible and move it towards the bird continually and slowly you will eventually succeed. This lesson must be repeated as often as possible - always taking care not to distress your bird - over a few days, or until the bird hops onto your finger, and perches there contentedly, as soon as this is placed into the cage.

3. Choosing Your Bird

Whether you wish to have a single pet canary in a cage or a breeding room filled with pairs of canaries of all varieties, your aim when buying birds should be to obtain the healthiest and best available. A weak and sickly pet bird will cause you disappointment and worry for years to come, while birds bred from inferior stock cannot be anything but inferior themselves.

You must decide on the variety of canary you want - whether this be for its color, shape or song. If song is important you have to be sure you choose a male bird; if color or shape is the most important feature you are advised to go to a canary show to look at the types of birds available and choose a variety that pleases you. But if you are like most pet canary owners your choice will probably just be for a colorful bird that sings nicely, a type readily available from pet shops or bird dealers - a bird that would never win a prize on a show bench, but one able to win the heart of a bird lover.

Sexing canaries is difficult for all but very experienced bird handlers - and they quite often make mistakes. Male birds are generally more bold and females rarely hold themselves as erect as males. Reputable pet shops and bird dealers will often offer replacement or money-back guarantees that the bird you buy is a male and will sing within, say, fourteen days. Unscrupulous dealers may try to sell off extra unwanted females to unwary buyers, so care must be taken.

Health and Age

When selecting your bird choose a young one which appears to be in good health and condition. Its feathers should be clean and well groomed, while the bird should be alert, with bright eyes. Birds which stand or squat on their perch with feathers or wings drooping, possibly with their head under a wing during the daytime, are obviously ill and should not be considered. Never buy a molting bird, as any changes in its routine could prove fatal at this stage. You will also find that molting canaries rarely sing.

A bird aged between seven and eight weeks is the best buy, even though the bird will not reach its peak singing abilities until it is between two and four years of age. Judging the age of a canary is difficult unless it has a closed and dated club ring on its leg. These leg rings are placed on birds when they are about eight days old and cannot be removed or replaced. Aged canaries usually have scaley legs, but these birds have been known to live for as long as fifteen years, and have an average lifespan of eight years, so the state of the legs is of little help in estimating the age of the birds.

Transporting Home

After you have bought your bird it is important to get it to its new home as promptly, and with as little disturbance, as possible. The bird seller should catch it quickly, without fuss, and put it in the cage or box for you to transport home. If you intend to carry the bird in a cage, make sure you have a thick cloth cover to drape over the bars while carrying it on the street, or in the car. Canaries are quite nervous birds and a sudden noise or movement could cause your bird to flutter against the bars of the cage in fright, possibly injuring itself.

Where the journey home will be over in a relatively short time - perhaps less than an hour - you should leave the food and water containers empty, or entirely out of the cage. The bird will be too disturbed to eat or drink and the contents will surely spill, making a mess in the cage. Any ladders or swings should also be left out, as they could fall around and frighten or injure your new pet. For longer trips you may need to place food and water in the cage for a short time, offering the bird a chance to eat or drink, then remove it again to avoid spillage.

If you have to, take your bird home in a small cardboard box. Avoid any suggestion by a dealer that you carry it home in a paper bag, as the risk of the bag tearing or the bird being crushed is too great. At home open the cage door and tear a corner from the box. Place the hole adjacent to the cage entrance and the bird will probably hop right into its new home unaided. If the bird is reluctant, put the box on a slight angle and tap it gently to encourage the bird to leave.

Once the bird is home and in its cage, along with filled food and water containers, avoid all temptation to make a fuss of it - at least for a day or two. Leave the bird alone in a quiet place so it can get used to its new surroundings undisturbed. Soon it will be confident enough to meet the humans who will play such an important part in its future life.

4. Feeding & General Care

At first glance, feeding a canary is a straightforward, clear cut process - a pack of birdseed from the local supermarket or pet shop and you have all you need! As far as it goes, this is right, but it doesn't really go far enough. Canaries need more than commercial seed mixes if they are to thrive and remain at the peak of health.

Seeds

First of all, the canary's basic seed mix must be fresh and clean. Dusty, dirty seed, perhaps fouled by vermin, is the source of much trouble. Old seed can become 'sour' and create digestive problems. The main part of a canary's diet is a small yellow seed, rounded at the middle and pointed at both ends, called canary seed. This seed forms the bulk of all canary mixes, making up at least two-thirds of those mixes. The next most important seed is rape, a small dark brown round seed rich in magnesium, lime, phosphoric acid and potash. If Roller Canaries are kept the proportion of this seed should be higher than that found in most mixes, so extra rape seed should be offered to the birds. This seed contains a high oil content.

Niger, a shiny, almost black, elongated seed, has a food value and oil content almost identical to rape seed. It is used widely by Red Factor breeders and is valuable in maintaining health, enriching plumage and restoring song to birds that have stopped singing. Breeders often use niger seed to combat the problem of egg binding in breeding hens. Maw, or poppy seed is very small and gray in color. It is high in oil content and is much loved by canaries. Readily digested, this seed combats constipation and diarrhea, but is reserved by many breeders for tonic or medicinal purposes.

Linseed, a pointed reddish seed, is often added to commercial canary mixes and is quite valuable during the molting season, as it gives a gloss to a bird's plumage. However, generally speaking, canaries are not too fond of its taste and will often eat very little of it from a seed mixture. Hulled oats are used by some breeders, particularly those who specialize in Red Factor Canaries, as a substitute for canary seed, especially in winter. Others use oats as an additive to seed mixes. This seed is believed to 'build' birds' bodies.

Hemp is a favorite seed of most canaries and is particularly valuable as a stimulating food during the breeding season. In many places, though, this seed is not commercially available - it is the seed of the marijuana plant! Where it is available, the seed has usually been devitalized so it cannot germinate. This process does not destroy the seeds' food value, or its appeal to canaries.

Tonic or treat seeds, contain various mixtures of some of the seeds already mentioned as well as more unusual ones such as dandelion, teasle, thistle, sesame, anise and some garden vegetable seeds. These are ideal for bringing birds into top condition during winter, after illness, or in preparation for bird shows. A small amount of tonic seed can be given to a bird every few days - either mixed with its normal ration or in a separate container.

Minerals

Equally important as any seed, though not a food, is grit - essential to a bird's digestion. Birds have no teeth and the grit enables food to be ground into digestible pieces after it enters the bird's crop. It must always be available to your bird. A number of types are available, some are mixtures of silica sand and shells whilst many contain valuable mineral supplements and charcoal. Ensure the grits you use are clean and free of fine dust. Grit can be purchased in handy packs from your local pet store or seed supplier.

Cuttlefish bone is also important to your bird's health, providing minerals and vitamins, in addition to keeping your bird's beak trimmed and in good condition. Cuttle bone can be collected on some beaches, but a safer way is to buy cleaned bone, often fitted with a metal clip for fixing it to the cage wire, from a pet shop. A valuable substitute for cuttle bone when this is not available is a vitaminized calcium block, also available from pet shops. Both cuttle bone and the compounded calcium blocks contain iodine, an important element in a bird's healthy growth.

Green-Food

Green vegetable foods play an important part in a canary's diet, providing essential vitamins and minerals. The variety of suitable greenstuff is wide - and can range from vegetables such as lettuce, spinach and silver beet to garden weeds like dandelion leaves. The most important thing is to ensure the greens are clean and free from any traces of chemicals such as weed killers or pesticides or fouling by wild birds or animals. Small gardens of sprouted grasses - including sprouted seeds from canary mixes - can be grown in trays or flower pots and placed in the bird's cage to provide a constant, fresh supply for your pet. Some pet shops sell dishes, ready planted with seed, which can be hung in the bird's cage after the seeds are dampened with water to start germination.

One important feature of feeding your bird green-foods is to offer as wide a variety as possible but offer small quantities at a time. Some people believe green-foods give birds diarrhea - and they will if the bird eats too much at a time. If a bird is deprived of green-foods for a time, then given an unlimited amount it will over-eat and digestive problems will result - just the same as if a small child is deprived of sweets, then given a free run in a chocolate shop. The answer to this is to give your bird a small quantity of greens every day, or at least two or three times a week.

Pieces of fruit such as apple, orange or banana, and serves of grated carrot will also be enjoyed by your bird. Fruit makes an important addition to the bird's diet in areas where green-foods are difficult to obtain during the winter. Care must be taken to remove both uneaten green-foods and fruit pieces before they become stale, wilted or moldy.

Soft Foods

Many canary breeders and fanciers feed their birds what is known in the hobby as 'soft' or 'egg food'. The most usual soft food is basically a biscuit meal with added hardboiled egg. Such foods can be mixed at home or bought as a powdered egg and biscuit mix from pet shops. This food can be added as an important rearing food for young canaries, but some fanciers continue to feed their birds a small amount of it about once a week, particularly during the winter. Many of the commercial soft foods available from pet shops also include wheat germ, yeast, powdered milk and mineral and vitamin additives, so their food value is high. Some canary keepers also give their birds occasional pieces of bread soaked in milk, but this works as a laxative, so should really be confined to medicinal use.

General Care

Cleanliness is the greatest factor in all animal husbandry - and with canaries the need is just as great. Canaries are hardy, healthy birds, but if their health is to be maintained they must not be subjected to any conditions which could lower their resistance to disease. A clean environment for your bird starts with its cage. A regular and thorough cleaning routine must be established and adhered to. Every few days - and certainly no less frequently than once a week - the cage must be cleaned of droppings, fallen feathers, seed husks and dust from the room. If sand sheets are used, this is an easy process, and a new sheet placed in position ensures a clean floor for your pet to walk on.

Perches should be scraped clean of any dropping and seed and water containers should be removed, emptied and washed in warm, soapy water before being refilled and replaced. The cleaning is completed by wiping the cage inside out with a damp cloth to remove any dust or dirt. Ensure the cage is left perfectly dry or the bird could suffer a chill.

Every day, seed dishes or hoppers must be checked to ensure there is plenty of seed available and not just a layer of seed husks. The digestive system and metabolism of birds is such that they will starve to death in a very short time - depending on the bird's age, but possibly in a period of less than twelve hours - if food is not available. An average canary weighs only about twenty grams, yet eats three-and-a-half grams of food each day, a high ratio of food to body weight. Water containers should be emptied, wiped with a cleaning cloth, then refilled each day. Stale and fouled water can quickly bring about intestinal disorders, even death.

While cleaning out the cage keep an eye open for red mites, parasites which suck the birds' blood and make their homes in cracks in woodwork and at the end of perches. If any traces of mite are found the bird, and its cage, will need treatment with a pesticide.

Bathing, particularly in hot weather, is important to canaries and is probably best carried out at least weekly, preferably before a cage clean-out, because quite a bit of water will be splashed around by the bird. Use water which is not icy cold so the bird does not suffer a chill. From time to time during warmer weather your bird will appreciate being placed outdoors. If this is possible make sure it is not left in direct sunlight for long unless an area of the cage is in shade. Birds have often died by being left in the hot sun.

If you keep several cock birds they may begin fighting together in winter and it could be necessary to separate them. Not all cock birds fight - but it does happen at times. Hens rarely fight and can be kept in small groups - up to five or so birds per cage if this is necessary or convenient. Be sure, however, not to overcrowd your birds, as this will lead to stress and could bring about health problems. Overcrowding also promotes fighting amongst birds and less aggressive individuals could be forced away from food, water or nesting space.

Birds intended as entries in shows should always be kept individually in cages, as this way there will be less danger of the birds' feathers being soiled or damaged. Show birds must be handled gently as often as possible to accustom them to humans at close quarters and to prepare them for the show bench. They should also spend some time every few weeks in a show cage, so the surroundings are not strange to them.

If your canaries are kept in a bird room it is a good idea to change the position of cages every few weeks. All bird rooms have good and poor locations, and by regularly changing their cage positions each bird has the advantage of a time in the best place, and none is constantly subjected to a less than ideal location.

One of the most important areas of regular care and maintenance of canaries - whether they are single pet birds or an aviary containing dozens of specimens - is simple observation of bird behavior. By watching your birds as often as you can you will quickly notice any abnormal signs which could indicate illness or some other problem - and the way the birds behave will usually enable an accurate diagnosis of the problem, which, if followed by rapid and accurate treatment, often remedies a potentially dangerous situation before any real damage is done.

5. Breeding & Exhibiting

Probably one of the most rewarding parts of bird keeping, in terms of interest and personal satisfaction, comes with breeding your own birds and for the canary fancier this can be achieved on a small scale with relatively little financial outlay. On making up your mind to breed canaries you must then decide on the type of housing you will use for the parents and their offspring. Some breeders use a single cage with one pair of birds, others use multiple cages, each containing a hen and mate a single cock bird to each hen in succession.

By far the most satisfactory way - also the easiest and most generally accepted - is to mate a pair of birds in a double cage fitted with a removable divider in the middle. These cages, usually wooden, can be bought ready-made from pet shops or made at home using a long box, two wire cage fronts and several extra pieces of wood and metal. One section of the double cage should contain a canary nest and both sections must have two or three perches. Metal, plastic, ceramic or wicker nests can be bought from pet shops.

Stock Purchase

Next you must decide on the variety of canary you wish to breed. You must make your mind up either to breed song birds or type birds, because attempts to compromise between the two rarely, if ever, really works. A. beginner, with no experience at breeding birds, may choose to pick from the free-breeding varieties like Red Factors, Border Fancies, Rollers, Glosters or Lizards, but excellent results can be obtained with a good pair of any variety.

Breeding stock can be bought at any time of the year, but the best birds are usually available in early to mid-winter, when many experienced breeders reduce their bird numbers. Many beginners wait until just before the breeding season to buy their birds, but this is not a good idea. At this time prices are highest, breeders are keeping their best birds for their own use, and there is no way of knowing how the birds have been kept in the vital time leading up to the breeding season.

The parent birds you choose should be the best you can afford. Although there can be no guarantees about the breeding potential of any bird, a reputable supplier will usually help and advise you with your purchases. If you join a canary club and talk to experienced breeders you will soon pick up

Breeding and
stock cages
for a canary
birdroom

quite a few valuable pointers - and fellow members may be able to supply you
with the birds you need, or at least advise you where to go to obtain suitable,
healthy birds.

Preparation for Breeding

When you get your birds home have the cage divider in place and put the hen
in one side and the cock in the other. Place the cage in a dry, airy and well lit
place, away from anything which could disturb the pair when they begin
breeding. Your birds will be ready to breed the following spring and a good
indicator of their impending readiness will be the nesting preparations of wild
birds. You must use the time between buying your birds and their mating to
ensure they are as physically fit as possible - and this means giving them a
nutritious and varied diet which includes a good seed mixture, fruit and
plenty of greens. Make sure both birds have plenty of fresh water and grit,
while the hen will benefit from extra calcium in the form of ground egg shell.

About one month before the breeding season starts both birds should have a
daily ration of soft food such as commercial egg food. As the breeding season
grows nearer the cock bird will call to the hen and she will answer him. The
cage divider should be replaced with an open-weave wire divider so the birds
can see each other. Nest building material - coconut fibre, horse hair, cotton
threads or a mixture obtained from a pet shop should be placed on the floor of
the hen's cage. The hen will probably start off playing with pieces of the
material at first, but then begin seriously constructing her nest. At this stage
she will accept food offered by the cock bird and her vent area will become

34

slightly enlarged and more reddish in color, indicating that she is ready to mate.

At this time the double cage and its contents should be treated against red mite, even if none have been noticed, as these can pose a danger to newly hatched chicks. The cage divider can now be removed and the birds allowed to contact each other. If they are allowed together before the hen is ready to mate some fighting could occur, and one of the birds could even be seriously injured. Watch the birds closely when they are first put together. Sometimes a hen which is obviously ready for mating will refuse to accept the male. If this happens place him back behind the cage divider and try to join the birds once more the next day - in the evening for preference. If she again rejects him you may have to obtain another male. If the birds get along together leave them alone and undisturbed.

The Eggs

The first egg could be laid about eight days after the birds are placed together, but it could take longer. When this egg is seen, carefully remove it and place it in a cloth-lined box and store it in a cool place. In its place put a dummy canary egg, obtainable from a pet shop, so the hen will return to the nest to lay subsequent eggs. A hen canary will lay between three and six eggs at about

Color variation in Border canaries at four weeks of age

daily intervals, with the average clutch numbering four eggs. The last egg to be laid is always darker in color than earlier eggs.

Remove the second and third eggs, replacing them with dummies, and store them with the first. When the fourth egg - or the last, darker, egg - is laid replace the stored eggs in the nest and remove the dummy eggs so incubation can start. By removing then replacing the eggs together, incubation of the whole clutch will be synchronized instead of the chicks hatching at intervals. This way each will have an equal chance of survival and development.

Some breeders move the cock bird back behind the cage divider after the second egg is laid, believing that he is likely to disturb the hen and encourage her to abandon the nest. Such breeders often allow him to return to the hen's section to help care for chicks, or place the chicks in his section for him to care for while the hen starts another brood. Other breeders leave the cock with the hen during the entire incubation and raising of the young, believing he plays an important role, attending to the hen, helping with the incubation while the hen is off the nest feeding and later with the raising of the young chicks. The beginner must decide which course of action to take, but it is probably best to leave the parent birds together until it is proved that the cock is distracting his mate. Hen canaries should be disturbed as little as possible during incubation, but if the bird is relatively tame you will do no harm by observing her behavior. You may notice her turn each egg several times a day to ensure even incubation.

Incubation normally lasts thirteen or fourteen days, but because some hens incubate poorly for the first few days, it can take longer. If no youngsters have appeared in, say, sixteen or seventeen days you should check to ensure the eggs are fertile. Do not pick them up in your fingers, but scoop up one at a time in a teaspoon and hold them against a light. Infertile eggs are transparent and can be discarded. In cases where all eggs are infertile you can give the pair a second chance to produce offspring, but if the same thing happens a second time it is likely that the cock is infertile and must be replaced. Egg development can be detected with a light after about five days' incubation.

Egg Binding

Egg binding is an internal condition which affects canary hens and can be brought about if birds are mated too early in the season or while they are still too young. Unmated hens, however, can also suffer the problem. Egg binding comes about when a hen is unable to pass an egg and its effects can range from minor distress to total prostration and eventual death of the bird. Symptoms of egg binding are distinctive. The hen usually squats on her nest, or the cage floor, with feathers fluffed and eyes partly closed. She will give every appearance of being in total discomfort.

Production of the egg and relief can sometimes be brought about in mild cases by placing the bird in a warm place — 27° to 32° C (80° to 90° F) — for an hour or two. If no egg results, a few drops of olive oil can be placed on the bird's vent to lubricate the area and make the egg's passage easier. Great care must be taken when handling an egg bound hen - firstly so the fragile egg shell is not shattered and secondly not to further weaken a bird already under great stress. The heat needed to help the bird can be produced by using an electric light globe or hot water bottle, but care must be taken to ensure the bird cannot be burnt by touching a hot surface.

Some bird keepers suggest gently massaging the abdomen of an egg bound hen to help her expel the egg, but this can be extremely dangerous when performed by an inexperienced person, as the pressure used and timing required is most important. It would be far wiser to seek veterinary assistance if an egg is not produced quickly using heat and olive oil. A veterinarian, using sterile surgical instruments, can usually collapse and remove a bound egg without endangering a hen's life. If a piece of broken shell perforates the bird's oviduct blood poisoning and death will result. Whatever treatment is decided on must be carried out quickly so the hen is not weakened beyond recovery.

Caring For the Chicks

When the young hatch they gain some nutrition from their yolk sac, which sustained them while in the egg, and the hen will not feed them very often for a day or so. After that she has a busy time and you will notice the chicks growing rapidly after about five days. Identification rings, obtainable from pet shops or canary societies, are slipped on the chicks' legs when they are about one week old.

During incubation, and for the first two days after the chicks have hatched, the hen can be given small quantities of egg food in addition to greens and mixed seed which includes a large percentage of maw and rape seed. After this, there must be a constant supply of egg food - but care must be taken that this is always fresh. Sour egg food will cause digestive upsets - even death - in young birds.

By the time the chicks are three weeks old they will have grown all their feathers - usually between the eighteenth and twenty-first day - and will leave the nest. They must, however, be left in the care of either the cock or hen for at least another week, and preferably ten or twelve days, because they will be unable to feed themselves properly.

If the cock bird is still in the hen's compartment after the chicks hatch you will have to watch him closely at first. Some cocks take their parental duties seriously and help the hen with the feeding, but others will attack, even kill, the chicks on sight.

Once the youngsters leave the nest the hen will begin to prepare for another brood or round - but as often as not she will feel this urge before her first chicks are ready to leave. Place another nest in the cage and supply the hen with more nesting material. As soon as she has finished her second nest allow

Just six of the many New Colored Canaries

38

the cock bird access to her. If he has been segregated from her and the young you should again pay careful attention to his attitude to the chicks. If the cock is at all aggressive towards them, or if the youngsters disturb the mating, as they often do, it is best to move the youngsters out of the cage for a while.

The first egg of the second brood will arrive quicker than the first of the initial clutch and the cock can be removed as soon as it arrives, as all eggs will be fertilised by then. Incubation and raising of the second brood will progress along the same lines as the first.

Care must be taken of the young birds after they leave the nest, as their beaks will be too soft to remove the husks from seed. They need a constant supply of egg food, plus a daily supply of rape seed soaked in water. The seed must be soaked daily and any uneaten grains must be removed at the end of each day so there is no danger of the birds eating any which has become affected by mildew. After a few days some canary mix should be added to the egg food and the youngsters should be given seeding grasses, a selection of green-food, fresh drinking water and bathing water.

When you are certain the youngsters are able to feed themselves they should be put into a cage by themselves - preferably a large flight cage or small aviary where they have plenty of room to fly about and develop strength. Continue

Gloster Canary hen about to feed her chicks

Bronze New Colored Canaries with their chicks

feeding the young birds egg food, at least until they finish their first molt, but in reduced amounts as they eat more and more seed. The first molt, which includes shedding head, body and neck feathers, but not wing or tail feathers, starts when the birds are about six weeks old and continues until they are about three months old. Some breeders continue feeding the young birds egg food throughout the summer, others think this is unnecessary.

You will probably need to know the sexes of your young canaries and some breeders believe this can be discovered by observing the birds in the nest, when they are as young as one week old. Cock birds, they say, are much bolder at this age and demand more food. Some breeders believe adult cocks feed young hens more often than they do cock chicks, while adult hens have a marked preference for feeding young cock birds. A far better way is to listen to the young birds. Cocks will begin singing attempts soon after they leave the nest. They will try to connect sounds together, quite unlike the soft twitterings of young hens.

If the young birds can spend their first year in an outdoor aviary, or at least a large indoor aviary, their development and health in future years will benefit. If you intend to breed more than one or two clutches of young birds from a single pair you would be well advised to keep comprehensive breeding records. Each breeding attempt should be fully recorded, with both parents identified, and full details of the resulting chicks, plus any other noteworthy happenings during the season.

40

Mating Rules

Simply 'breeding canaries' is often quite a different matter from breeding top specimens of any canary variety, and if you wish to breed show birds you should first learn to recognize the standards set for each breed. The rules of inheritance of characteristics must be followed to ensure the desired traits, and no others, are passed to the offspring. Breeders, for instance, mate yellow canaries to buffs, which result in fifty per cent of each feather type. These birds are of better quality than birds produced by yellow/yellow or buff/buff matings. Crested birds are bred with uncrested birds to avoid a lethal gene coupling often found when two cresteds are mated together. If the lethal gene is present the chicks die, either in the egg or soon after they hatch; if the gene is not present in a crested/crested breeding, the crests of the offspring are generally below standard.

Another lethal gene comes into action when dominant white canaries - a mutation which has been introduced into most standard varieties - are bred together, so breeders satisfy themselves with fifty per cent whites resulting from white/normal matings. There are also a number of sex-linked characteristics found in canaries - some only found in males, others only in females.

Red-orange Red Factors mated with apricot-type Red Factors are generally found to produce the best offspring, while Lizard Canary breeders have found that they produce superior birds by mating gold-types with silvers. Roller Canary breeders usually depend on inbreeding or line breeding - mating related birds - to ensure they keep and improve their birds' singing abilities.

Exhibiting

The logical conclusion of a breeding program is to establish its value in competition with others, in short, exhibiting one's stock. Probably the best way for a beginner to learn the finer points of canary care and breeding is to join a canary club or society - either one interested in canaries in general or a specialist group concerned with one particular variety. By attending meetings, listening to lectures and talking with fellow members the new bird keeper will have access to invaluable information and expertise. A feature of almost all such societies is the regular bird show. By attending and entering birds in these shows a new breeder will soon learn how their breeding program is progressing and see first hand the standards they should be trying to achieve. Most shows have sections for newcomers to the hobby of canary breeding.

Unlike in budgerigars, canaries do not have a single style and size of show cage. Each variety has its own, designed to standards set by the national governing society for that variety. Exhibitors must provide their own show cage and they will also need a carrying case, used to transport their birds, in their cages, to shows. Before reaching the show season, exhibitors often put in

41

Trio of Gloster Canaries about three weeks old

many hours preparing their birds to meet the judge. While the birds are still young they are trained to enter a show cage and display themselves in the best manner of their variety. A nervous or fluttering bird cannot be properly assessed by the judge. Rollers must be taught to sing on cue in strange surroundings.

A few days before a show, many exhibitors hand wash their birds to ensure plumage is clean and attractive. The wash must be carried out early enough for the feathers to tighten up and regain their bloom prior to the show.

Canary societies vary in their specifications about show cage floor coverings. Some require a layer of canary seed, others blotting paper and some oat husks. If plain canary seed is used it will also serve as a food supply for the show birds. If other material is used the canaries on show must be given a food supply adequate for them during the whole exhibition. The show cage also needs a removable drinking water dispenser.

Birds can be left at or sent to a show, to be cared for by stewards, and their owners need never attend - but a beginner can gain valuable experience by entering and attending every show possible. Many beginners have been pleasantly surprised by the results their birds achieved in competition - but all birds are judged on their relevant merits according to the standards of their variety. First prizes may seem elusive, but the experience gained at shows can help a breeder reach the top. After a show, exhibited birds might appear tired and run down, but a cool drink, bath and a serve of favorite seeds will soon have them back in good form.

6. Health

Although many people believe that canaries are delicate birds, this is not so. They are remarkably hardy and if housed and cared for properly health problems are likely to be few and, unless you are unfortunate, restricted to minor ailments that are easily overcome.

Disease prevention being better than cure, it behooves all bird keepers to be particularly fastidious over cleanliness of cages, birdrooms and aviaries. Most health problems arise directly as a result of dirty, and usually damp, conditions, fouled or sour food, lack of sufficient daylight or fresh ventilation. Access to flights or food stores by vermin, or even local birds such as sparrows, are further means by which the army of unwanted creepy crawlies gain entry into your bird's home.

Owners of single caged pet canaries should never have major problems simply because keeping the cage and food cupboard clean is not really a difficult task. Where many birds are kept in birdrooms and aviaries (especially the former) things can be more difficult. If exposed floorboards are not covered with linoleum or similar, parasitic populations can build up because disinfecting is almost impossible. Birdrooms converted from rooms in your home should be carefully planned in order that light and ventilation is good. Food bins should be such that they can be well sealed and cleaned. All utensils must be kept thoroughly washed and of non rusting material. You are well advised to have a supply of water to birdrooms and aviaries, if possible, as you will need to wash your hands after handling birds from different cages and especially after handling sick birds.

When building aviaries, try to avoid any construction that might prove difficult to get at when completed - such places are guaranteed to attract parasites and bacterial fungi. Keep your netting in good repair so that wild birds and mice cannot gain entry. A hospital cage is useful for canary breeders - and the further it is away from your main stock the better. Likewise, an isolation cage is advised in order that you can keep newly acquired birds away from your stock until you are sure they are not carrying any disease. Mounds of garden debris, especially grass cuttings, in the vicinity of an aviary can be very bad news, yet is an easily overlooked source of trouble.

Pet owners should keep a careful check on the cage corners and underneath metal cleaning trays as well as under the over-turned metal cage edges. All these areas are prone to get damp when the bird is bathing, or after you have washed the cage, and as a result may well start to rust and in so doing create a safe haven for mites.

It would be safe to say that if you ever have need of detailed and extensive knowledge of avian ailments then you have real problems, but none-the-less some information on the most likely causes of trouble may help in spotting and treating such.

Symptoms

Broadly speaking, most ailments can be divided into three categories; these being parasitic infections, intestinal and respiratory problems, and broken limbs or cuts. The latter are self evident and can be specifically treated but the first two groups can cover a multitude of cause and effect situations. Many can be interacting, in that the onset of one problem directly leads to the incidence of another. It is not possible to attribute a particular symptom to a specific disease as often numerous ailments may have much the same symptoms, thus making good diagnosis difficult.

A sickly bird is easily spotted as it will sit hunched on its perch with its feathers obviously ruffled; it may or may not have difficulty in breathing and its appetite will most certainly be affected. Its droppings may be greenish and its eyes will be partly closed and possibly with a discharge. Some birds may vomit, though this is not always indicative of ill health - only if in association with other obvious symptoms mentioned. A bird unduly pecking at its feathers, or any that appear very restless or quarrelsome, may also have one or more complaints.

Remedies

Treating a sick bird is really a question of a process of elimination of likely causes. At the first sign of illness the bird should be isolated from others and placed in a warm room or hospital cage. Heat, together with a quiet environment, can work wonders and its first effect is usually to induce drinking - and antibiotics can thus be given via the water. Once the bird is isolated, the beginner is advised to consult a local experienced breeder or veterinarian who may well diagnose the source of the problem. There are many commercial medicines available from pet shops which will help cure coughs, chills, minor diarrhea and the like, whilst mite and lice are easily eradicated these days with the many aerosol sprays or powders. In all cases one should read, and follow, manufacturers' directions carefully.

Attention to the diet will often be helpful and is dealt with under the specific problem in the following text. Whatever the cause, you are recommended to thoroughly clean the bird's accommodation whilst it is undergoing treatment, and be sure to 'harden' the bird off once it is clearly well again. By this is meant that it should be returned gradually to its regular diet and to its normal room or aviary temperature, thus reducing the risk of inducing a soft molt or a chill.

Likely Problems

Cold and Chill: These are caused by sudden changes in temperature, shock, injury, during a molt or by incorrect or insufficient food. In all cases they result in body stress which affects the lungs. Sufferers should be placed in heated quarters and common remedies include a pinch of Epsom Salts in the water, a drop of whisky and even a smear of inhalation compound on the bird's nostrils. Veterinary prescriptions may be added to the drinking water.

Intestinal Disorders: Swollen abdomens, loose and stained droppings, loss of weight, obesity, discharge from the beak or nostrils and many other symptoms would all indicate intestinal malfunction and veterinary help is advised. Internal worms of many species may be found in most birds but their importance in disease is only vaguely understood. However, there is little doubt that infestations within an already ill bird can do only harm. Most worms require an intermediate host and the most likely one will be an earthworm or one of many insects. Aviary birds are thus more likely to be susceptible. Whenever internal disorders are suspected modify diet to eradicate the chance of worm hosts being included.

Treatment for intestinal worms is to put measured amounts of commercially available bird worming compounds, containing the chemical piperazine adipate, in the bird's drinking water. As with most parasite and disease conditions, the bird cage must be thoroughly cleansed to avoid reinfection.

Lice: These are tiny wingless insects that live and feed on the bird's body, leaving it only to attach themselves to another bird. There are many species but all have much the same effect in that they create irritation which causes the bird to unduly preen itself to the point that baldness can occur. They can multiply very quickly, especially where birds are together in cramped quarters. Close inspection of your bird will establish their existence. They are easily dealt with by any of the modern insecticides sold for their removal. Check that the one you use has a binding action that will last long enough to kill any larvae that may still be on the bird. All housing should be treated at the same time to prevent re-infestation.

Red Mite: Unlike lice, red mite spend only short periods on the bird - gorging themselves on its blood before returning to the safety of a crevice. They attack the host during the night. They are small gray arthropods which appear red after feeding. They can reduce a bird's stamina very considerably and may cause a hen to abandon her nest of chicks. With increased debility, host birds are more likely to fall victim to lice and disease. It is essential that all accommodation be treated with the appropriate spray and even be re-painted with an impregnated acaricide paint. Nesting material should be burned. As red mite can survive off the host for up to a year, keep a very close watch for them at all times — they can best be seen at night in flashlight when they will appear as red specks on perches, cage floors and the birds.

Air Sac Mite: Canaries are among the many species of birds which can be infected by air sac mite, an infection which results in loss of condition, breathing problems, ruffled feathers and coughing. The mite can eventually cause the death of a bird if the problem is not treated. Remedies, usually containing malathion, can be bought from pet shops and treatment involves puffing the material into a closed box containing the bird so some of the powder is inhaled. A series of treatments at monthly intervals is usually necessary.

Respiratory Problems: Any bird that sneezes, has difficulty in breathing, or has a discharge from its eyes, nostrils or beak or displays a loss of appetite in association with these symptoms may be suffering from one of many respiratory complaints. Such birds should be isolated and veterinary advice sought without delay.

Strokes: Both old and very young birds may be subject to strokes, fits, convulsions or epilepsy type behavior. In all cases they should be transferred to a quiet, dimly lit room where the temperature should be between 15° - 21° C (60° - 70° F). Some will appear normal in a short time whilst others may take a few hours to come round. A clinical examination is needed to determine the cause which can be through vitamin deficiency, mild poisoning, obesity, lack of oxygen, fright or brain damage. Quite often poorly fed pets are the most likely to suffer convulsion-like behavior. The feeding of 'unnatural' tit-bits over a long period can result in increased blood-pressure in pets and if the bird is then startled by a cat, or a noise, this creates stress, panic and excessive movement, which may result in temporary oxygen loss to the brain - thus the apparent fit.

Ring-band Leg Damage: If your bird is fitted with a closed metal leg ring, be especially watchful that this always remains loose fitting. Some canaries, as they age, may develop thick legs where the ring might restrict the blood flow. Swollen legs after injury could be likewise at risk. In severe cases legs can literally fall off if the ring is too tight. Veterinary surgery can be used in cases where there is a need to remove the ring.

Broken Limbs: These can be caused by fighting, getting caught in netting, or by sudden fright - causing the bird to crash into posts or such. An injured bird should be placed in isolation and where there are few objects to flutter into. Perches should be removed or placed very low in the cage. Minor breaks will heal by themselves and major fractures should be referred to veterinarians. Splints are possible but often unsuccessful as they cause the bird to panic making matters worse.

Overgrown Claws and Beaks: Canaries' claws and beaks which become overgrown will require trimming and care must be taken not to sever veins during this operation or your bird could bleed to death. If the upper beak has grown too long, and overhangs the lower beak, carefully trim off the excess using sharp nail scissors, or a pair of special trimming scissors obtainable from some pet shops. Birds with overgrown claws should be held under a strong light so the veins or quick can be easily seen extending from the feet into the claws. Any trimming should stop at least one mm away from a vein. Properly done, trimming a canary's claws or beak will be no more painful for the bird than trimming your own fingernails is for you. Many birds will need to have their claws trimmed once a year, some may need it more often.

Hospital Cages

Whilst special hospital cages have much to recommend them, prospective owners of these should exercise a degree of caution both in their construction and use. It is essential that the thermostat controlling the temperature is sensitive to increase or decrease beyond the desired level otherwise there is a raised risk of chilling through fluctuations in heat. The most beneficial temperature range is 22° - 28° C (72° - 82° F). Adequate ventilation is a must. It will be appreciated that in a raised temperature many bacteria will multiply at a greater rate therefore such a cage must be sterilized after each occupant - if electric bulb type ones are used this aspect can be difficult. Most commercially available cages are small and this means the bird is unable to escape the direct heat when it becomes uncomfortable. If overhead light bulbs are the source of heat then the bird is unable to rest properly. Consideration should be given to the use of infra-red heat in a cage large enough for the bird to move away from the heat as it requires. The comfort of the patient is your guide to the success of the cage.

Variegated (left) and clear buff Norwich Canaries

7. Molting

At some stage each summer all canaries undergo their annual molt - and although this is a perfectly natural phase, during which the birds' feathers are shed and replaced progressively over a period of six to eight weeks, it is a period fraught with danger for a bird which is poorly fed and improperly cared for. Each year many otherwise healthy canaries die because their care and diet has not prepared their bodies for the rigors of the annual molt, following as it does, hard on the heels of the breeding season.

Not all canaries molt at exactly the same time. Some will begin earlier than others, some will complete theirs quickly, while others continue in molt for quite a while, but all canaries molt in an orderly, defined pattern which allows only a few feathers to be shed at a time so the birds retain their powers of flight throughout the whole period. The first feathers are shed from the wings and the bird's underside, then the molt gradually extends over the whole body, finishing at the head and neck. New feathers develop from the same skin

Variegated Blue
White Gloster
Canary consort

48

depression from which the old ones are shed. Growing feathers are nourished by a vein which enters the feather base.

Male canaries either stop singing or sing very little during this period and, in the early stages, birds of both sex appear sleepy and lazy, even during the day.

The most important factor in ensuring a canary successfully completes its molt in good health, and emerges from it with attractive, fresh plumage, is an adequately rich and varied diet. Feathers are almost pure protein in composition, so protein-rich seeds should be given in addition to the bird's normal staple diet. Such seeds include rape, linseed, maw, vetch and niger. Daily, or at least every second day, molting birds should receive a small serve of soft egg food.

Although each bird must receive a generous ration of food each day during its' molt, care must be taken that they are not overfed, as a lack of exercise could result in them becoming too fat and later suffering liver problems. A plentiful supply of fresh, uncontaminated green-food should also be available to the birds during this time. In addition to important vitamins and minerals, vegetable matter also contains the chemicals necessary to form the yellow pigment which colors their feathers. Useful greens include lettuce, spinach, seeding grasses, chickweed and thistle flowers.

Birds which are color fed to give them the chemicals required to manufacture their feather pigmentations should receive their color food throughout the molting period. Such varieties include Red Factor, Yorkshire, Norwich and Lizards - but remember that color feeding simply intensifies the color already bred genetically into a bird and will not produce color in a bird which is naturally pale. Breeders have experimented with many color foods over the years, but most now rely on commercial preparations available from pet shops and the use of one of these preparations is easier and more likely to be successful than by following any home-made recipe. Color food is usually added to a bird's soft food according to the manufacturer's directions.

During the molting period birds should be kept in airy conditions, free from drafts - and care should be taken to ensure they do not receive a severe fright, as this could halt or slow down the process. Molting birds are not sick, they are simply undergoing a natural function, but they are generally more sensitive than usual at this time.

Four or five birds can be kept together in a roomy cage during this period but care must be taken against overcrowding, and a watch should be kept to ensure none develops the habit of pulling feathers out of a cage mate. If this habit goes unchecked it could continue after the molt has ended. Any offending birds should be isolated immediately. Birds intended for showing are also best kept in a cage by themselves so their feathers develop as perfectly as possible, without any danger of being damaged or dirtied.

Molting birds should be given access to a bath as often as possible - preferably every day, but at least several times a week. Bathing helps the shedding of old

New
Colored
Canaries

feathers and the preening it encourages improves the growth and formation of
new feathers. Allow the birds to bathe early in the day and ensure they are
properly dry before they roost if they bathe in the afternoon, or chills could
result.

Continue feeding the birds a rich and generous diet for a few weeks after the
end of the molt to ensure they return to their peak condition as quickly as
possible. At this time a bird's feathers will be extremely soft and have a loose
appearance. After about a week the feathers become more compact and
harden so they are less prone to damage.

Some canaries suffer from a condition known as soft molt, which involves a
shedding of feathers outside the normal season. The condition is triggered off
by a sudden temperature change, such as happens if a bird is kept in a warm
room for several weeks and is then suddenly placed in an area which is much
cooler. The bird could well react by stopping its song and going into a partial
or soft molt. The result can be identical if the bird is suddenly moved from a
cool room into one which is much warmer. The way to avoid this problem is
to avoid moving your bird from room to room if there is a large temperature
difference.

Feathers which become damaged or broken outside the molting period can be
plucked out. This sometimes promotes growth of a replacement feather,
depending on a number of factors, but the feather will certainly be replaced
during the next molt. If the vein in a damaged feather is broken the bird could
bleed profusely for a time, but the bleeding stops once the feather is plucked.
Canaries have been known to bleed to death through damaged feathers,
although instances of this are quite rare.

50

8. Taming and Training

Many canaries are never tamed and do not receive a moment's training in their lives. Others, like Roller Canaries, are taught until they reach the peak of their singing ability, while show birds are educated so they are at ease and pose well on a show bench. Pet canaries, on the other hand, are often tamed and trained on a continuing basis from the day they are bought until they finally die of old age.

Much of the fun of owning a canary can come from both the taming and training process - and the response a gentle, caring owner can get from their bird would surprise most people, particularly those who look on canaries as pretty but unintelligent little creatures.

The training of a Roller cock should start as soon as the young bird is weaned and isolated from hens and other birds. It should be placed in a room with other young cocks and at least one teacher - an adult Roller cock which is an excellent performer, capable of perfect delivery of the variety's songs, or tours. A well-bred young Roller will teach itself to sing well, but training is necessary if the bird is to reach its full potential.

Beautiful head study of the "Wee Gem" - the Gloster Canary corona

The ideal Roller classroom is darkened slightly so the young birds can concentrate without distraction on the only thing they hear - the song of their teacher. As the young birds learn their songs the bird keeper listens closely and removes any birds which utter shrill or harsh sounds, or those that repeat some passages too infrequently, so these faults will not be learnt by other birds. At first all the youngsters are placed in a large flight cage together, but later they are placed in individual training cages so each can be listened to and observed more closely. This separation usually takes place after the birds' first molt.

A full training program is time consuming, complicated and quite demanding. Often only a very small percentage of birds which start the program remain and go on to Roller exhibitions. The remainder are culled out as unsuitable along the way. A training graduate will usually begin singing for an exhibition judge as soon as its cage is opened.

Type Birds

The training that goes into preparing other canary varieties for showing is minor compared with that required for Rollers. The first step, which starts as soon as the birds are weaned, is to get them accustomed to show cages, and then to have them enter the cages on command. This is usually done by placing a show cage near the young birds' cage, with the cage doors adjoining and open so the birds have ready access to either cage.

Once the bird is relaxed perched on your finger it will probably be willing to step on the palm of your hand and eat seed or other food you place there. When you want a released bird to return to its cage, simply get it to perch on your hand and carry it to the cage. While the bird is out loose let it hop on your hand, then place it on your shoulder, head or the rim of a pair of spectacles.

From time to time you will need to catch and hold your canary in your hand - to trim its claws, dose it with medicine, or just to put it back in its cage if it refuses to return perched on your finger. To do this place the palm of your hand across the bird's back when its wings are in the folded position, then grasp it tightly with your fingers. This method will ensure you do not crush the bird or apply pressure to its delicate neck and the bird cannot injure itself by flapping its wings or struggling violently. After being held gently a few times the bird will learn to relax in your hand - but will probably never really enjoy it.

If you plan to let your canary out of its cage regularly you should set a routine so your pet does not escape. Lock all doors, or tell everyone in the house the bird is free. Ensure all openings are blocked and electrical appliances are switched off. If all the foregoing advice is heeded you can look forward to many years of pleasure and companionship with your canary, and enjoy the benefit of his beautiful song.